ANCIENT EGYPT: PYRAMIDS AND PHARAOHS

Ancient Egypt was a thriving civilization, lasting over 3,000 years.

Ancient Egyptian pyramids are the most well known pyramid structures. There are around 138 Egyptian pyramids.

Most Ancient
Egyptian
pyramids
were built as
tombs for
Pharaohs and
their families.

The pyramids of Egypt are all built to the west of the Nile River. This is because the western side was associated with the land of the dead.

The Pharaohs
of Ancient
Egypt were
the supreme
leaders of
the land.

A Pharaoh
was the most
important
and powerful
person in the
kingdom.

The Pharaohs
wore a crown
that had an
image of
the cobra
goddess. Only
the Pharaoh
was allowed
to wear the
cobra goddess.

Pharaohs built great tombs for themselves so they could live well in the afterlife.